I Like Biographies!

Read About
Neil
Armstrong

Stephen Feinstein

Enslow Elementary
an imprint of
Enslow Publishers, Inc.

40 Industrial Road   PO Box 38
Box 398   Aldershot
Berkeley Heights, NJ 07922   Hants GU12 6BP
USA   UK

http://www.enslow.com

Words to Know

astronaut—A person who travels in space.

license—A card or paper showing that a person has permission to do something, such as drive or fly.

mission—A job a person wants to accomplish.

orbit—The path followed by something in space as it circles around something else (such as a planet).

pilot—Someone who flies a plane or a spaceship.

space suit—A suit that makes it possible for a person to live in space.

Enslow Elementary, an imprint of Enslow Publishers, Inc.

Enslow Elementary® is a registered trademark of Enslow Publishers, Inc.

Copyright © 2005 by Enslow Publishers, Inc.

Library of Congress Cataloging-in-Publication Data

Feinstein, Stephen.
    Read about Neil Armstrong / Stephen Feinstein.
        p. cm. — (I like biographies!)
    Includes bibliographical references and index.
    ISBN 0-7660-2593-4
    1. Armstrong, Neil, 1930–   —Juvenile literature. 2.
Astronauts—United States—Biography—Juvenile literature.
3. Project Apollo (U.S.)—Juvenile literature. 4. Space
flight to the moon—Juvenile literature. I. Title. II. Series.
    TL789.85.A75F45 2005
    629.45'0092—dc22
            [B]
                            2004013170

Printed in the United States of America

10 9 8 7 6 5 4 3 2 1

Illustration Credits: National Aeronautics and Space Administration (NASA), pp. 1, 3, 5, 15, 17, 19, 21, 22; Ohio Historical Society, pp. 7, 9, 11, 13.

Cover Illustration: National Aeronautics and Space Administration (NASA).

Contents

Neil Armstrong was born in Ohio on August 5, 1930. As a little boy, Neil liked to watch planes take off and land at the airport. He wished he could ride in one.

When Neil was six, his wish came true. His father took him to see a new plane called the *Tin Goose*. The pilot offered to take Mr. Armstrong and Neil up for a short ride in the sky.

Neil Armstrong grew up to be one of America's most famous pilots.

The *Tin Goose* rolled down the runway and rose into the air. Soon it was high above the ground. Neil could see houses and cars down below that looked like tiny toys. Sometimes the plane tilted from side to side. Sometimes it dropped suddenly, and Neil felt like his stomach was in his mouth. But he enjoyed every minute.

When he was a little boy, Neil loved to watch planes. One day he got to go for a plane ride. He was so excited he could hardly believe what was happening.

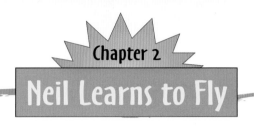

As Neil grew older, he became more and more interested in flying. He built model airplanes and read about airplanes.

Neil even began to have dreams about flying. In his dreams, Neil floated high above the ground, flying like a bird. He was always sorry when he woke up and knew it was just a dream.

These are planes like the *Tin Goose*, in which Neil had his first airplane ride.

When Neil was fifteen, he decided to become a pilot. He took flying lessons on a tiny plane. Neil's teacher showed him how to take off and land, how to climb and swoop down. Neil got his student pilot's license on his sixteenth birthday.

Neil played the baritone horn in the school band. Here he is in his band uniform.

During the Korean War, Neil was a pilot in the U.S. Navy. He learned to fly jet fighters. From 1950 to 1952, he flew seventy-eight missions off the deck of a ship called the U.S.S. *Essex*.

In 1956, Neil married Jan Shearon. Later they had three children.

Here is Neil's wife, Jan, with two of their children, Mark and Eric.

13

After the war, Neil worked as a test pilot. He flew many kinds of new jets and rocket planes. In 1962, NASA chose Neil for the Apollo program. They wanted to send an American to the moon. Neil trained for four years to become an astronaut. On March 16, 1966, Neil flew his first space mission around Earth.

Neil trained to be an astronaut with NASA, the National Aeronautics and Space Administration. Here he is with two other astronauts, Michael Collins in the center and Buzz Aldrin on the right.

On July 16, 1969, *Apollo 11* blasted off. Neil Armstrong flew with Buzz Aldrin and Mike Collins. They reached the moon in four days and went into orbit around it.

Apollo 11 had two parts. Neil and Buzz went into the *Eagle*, the moon-landing craft. Mike stayed on the command ship *Columbia*. The *Eagle* pulled away and landed on the moon.

This is the *Apollo 11* spacecraft blasting off for the moon with the three astronauts aboard.

Neil was the first to step down onto the dusty surface of the moon. He was wearing a space suit. Neil looked up at the black sky and saw Earth. It looked very small.

Neil said, "That's one small step for a man, one giant leap for mankind." Millions of people watched the landing on TV. Neil and Buzz put an American flag on the moon.

Neil took this picture of Buzz standing next to the flag. It was specially made to stand out straight, since there is no wind on the moon.

The three *Apollo 11* astronauts returned safely to Earth. Everyone welcomed them as heroes.

Neil left NASA in 1971. He taught space science at the University of Cincinnati. Now he lives on his farm in Ohio. But we will always remember Neil Armstrong's courage as the first person to set foot on the moon.

There were parades all over the world to welcome the three astronauts. Here they are in Australia.

Timeline

1930—Neil is born in Ohio on August 5.

1946—Neil gets his pilot's license.

1950–1952—Neil is a jet fighter pilot in the U.S. Navy during the Korean War.

1962—Neil is chosen to be an astronaut.

1966—Neil makes his first space flight.

1969—On July 20, Neil becomes the first person to walk on the moon.

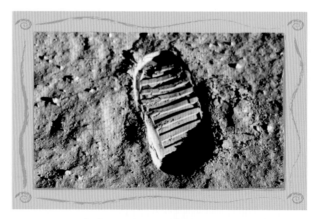

A footprint on the moon.

Learn More

Books

Brown, Dan. *One Giant Leap: The Story of Neil Armstrong.* Boston: Houghton Mifflin, 1998.

Hehner, Barbara. *First on the Moon: What It Was Like When Man Landed on the Moon.* New York: Hyperion Books for Children, 1999.

Lassieur, Allison. *Astronauts.* New York: Children's Press, 2000.

Streissguth, Thomas. *Neil Armstrong.* Mankato, Minn.: Bridgestone Books, 2003.

Suen, Anastasia. *Man on the Moon.* New York: Viking, 1997.

Internet Addresses

Landing on the Moon: A 30th Anniversary
<http://kids.msfc.nasa.gov/News/1999/News-Apollo11.asp>

World Almanac for Kids: Space
<http://www.worldalmanacforkids.com/explore/space.html>

Index